Don't Be a Bully

By Frances Nagle

 Gareth Stevens
PUBLISHING

first
concepts

A bully is someone who tries to hurt another person or make them feel bad.

23

Please visit our website, www.garethstevens.com. For a free color catalog of all our high-quality books, call toll free 1-800-542-2595 or fax 1-877-542-2596.

Library of Congress Cataloging-in-Publication Data

Nagle, Frances.
Don't be a bully / by Frances Nagle.
p. cm. — (Minding our manners)
Includes index.
ISBN 978-1-4824-1620-6 (pbk.)
ISBN 978-1-4824-1621-3 (6-pack)
ISBN 978-1-4824-1619-0 (library binding)
1. Bullying — Juvenile literature. I. Title.
BF637.B85 N34 2015
302.3—d23

First Edition

Published in 2015 by
Gareth Stevens Publishing
111 East 14th Street, Suite 349
New York, NY 10003

Copyright © 2015 Gareth Stevens Publishing

Designer: Andrea Davison-Bartolotta
Editor: Kristen Rajczak

Photo credits: Cover, p. 1 (main) stefanolunardi/Shutterstock.com; cover, back cover, p. 1 (blue background) Eky Studio/Shutterstock.com; p. 3 Fuse/Thinkstock; p. 5 Twin Design/Shutterstock.com; p. 7 LWA/The Image Bank/Getty Images; p. 9 BananaStock/Thinkstock; p. 11 Craig Dingle/E+/Getty Images; p. 13 Stephen Coburn/Shutterstock.com; p. 15 Cultra RM/Anni Engel/Collection Mix: Subjects/ Getty Images; p. 17 JillianSuzanne/iStock/Thinkstock; p. 19 Jupiterimages/Pixland/Thinkstock; p. 21 Jupiterimages/Creatas/Thinkstock; p. 23 iofoto/Shutterstock.com.

Printed in the United States of America

CPSIA compliance information: Batch #CW15GS: For further information contact Gareth Stevens, New York, New York at 1-800-542-2595.

Some bullies hurt others by hitting or pushing them.

5

Other bullies
say mean things.

There are many reasons why bullies hurt people. They might want to fit in.

9

Bullies try to feel important by making others feel bad.

11

Bullies often pick
on people
who are different.

13

A bully might not
know how to deal
with problems
in a healthy way.

15

It is okay to feel
angry or hurt.
But there is no
good reason
to bully someone.

17

Take time to calm down. Then, talk about any problems you have.

Think about how
you would feel if you
were being bullied.

Stand up for those who are being bullied. You will feel good helping others!